The
Rewarding Practice
of
Journal Writing

Books by James E. Miller

Welcoming Change
Discovering Hope in Life's Transitions

Autumn Wisdom
Finding Meaning in Life's Later Years

The Caregiver's Book
Caring for Another, Caring for Yourself

When You Know You're Dying
12 Thoughts to Guide You Through the Days Ahead

One You Love Is Dying
12 Thoughts to Guide You on the Journey

When You're Ill or Incapacitated / When You're the Caregiver

What Will Help Me? / How Can I Help?

How Will I Get Through the Holidays?
12 Ideas for Those Whose Loved One Has Died

Winter Grief, Summer Grace
Returning to Life After a Loved One Dies

A Pilgrimage Through Grief
Healing the Soul's Hurt After Loss

Helping the Bereaved Celebrate the Holidays
A Sourcebook for Planning Educational and Remembrance Events

Effective Support Groups
How to Plan, Design, Facilitate, and Enjoy Them

A Little Book for Preachers
101 Ideas for Better Sermons

With Tom Golden

When A Man Faces Grief / A Man You Know Is Grieving

The
Rewarding Practice
of
Journal Writing

A Guide for Starting and Keeping
Your Personal Journal

James E. Miller

WILLOWGREEN®
PUBLISHING

To John Peterson,
an honest friend, an unselfish support.

Nothing I have ever created or written is really mine. This book, despite its personal tone, is no exception. Clare Barton, Sue Devito, Jennifer Levine, Lyn Miletich, Bernie Miller, and John Peterson all share ownership, having improved the manuscript with their wise and thoughtful feedback.

This is as good a place as any to make my confession: I've taken small liberties with a handful of quotations included in these pages. I choose to believe the original writers would want to be as gender-inclusive as possible, were they alive today.

Willowgreen Publishing
PO Box 25180
Fort Wayne, Indiana 46825
219/424-7916

Library of Congress Catalogue
Card Number: 98-90456

ISBN 1-885933-28-2

*We write to heighten
our awareness of life.
We write to taste life twice,
in the moment and in retrospection.
We write to be able to transcend our life,
to reach beyond it,...
to teach ourselves to speak with others,
to record the journey into the labyrinth.*

ANAÏS NIN

Introduction

"I sit down here to write and I wonder why I am doing this. I've tried doing the same thing before and it's lasted only two or three days. I look upon this writing as a kind of discipline—a way of thinking things through, coming to know where I am, venting feelings that often go unvented. To do it on paper is laborious for me, and so final. But I am aware that my perspective is often not adequate. So I do this."

I wrote those words on the first page of a black hardbound journal the third week of January, 1972. I was 27 years old. As it turned out, the practice I started that cold morning lasted more than a few days. It's been 26 years and I'm still writing. Not every day, but most days. I don't know how I could have gone through all those years if I had not journaled regularly.

I've filled a small shelf of books with my thoughts and feelings. Sometimes the handwriting appears slow and even, as if I had carefully formed the ideas. At other times the words have been penned hastily, as much scribbling as anything else. Entries appear in blue and black and red ink, depending upon which writing instrument was closest at hand. Once when I learned that a program I had started for elder adults had just received a critical federal grant, I wrote *"Got the money!"* in giant crayon lettering across two full pages.

These books overflow with my life—the ups and downs of my work, the ins and outs of my closer relationships, the ways I succeeded and failed as a husband, my experiences first as a young father and later as an older one. Agony is recorded in those pages when I left a career I never planned to leave, when I went through a separation and divorce, when a life-threatening illness struck someone I love deeply. Deep joy is also documented there. So are some memorable adventures and my full share of dreams-come-true.

Some of what's written is boring—rambling thoughts, repetitious feelings, and wordy reflections that aren't nearly as profound as they once seemed. But taken as a whole, what I wrote on that first page half a lifetime ago is true: my journaling has given me perspective. It's also educated me, encouraged me, pushed me, and freed me. So this will not surprise you: I believe in the value of journaling. That's why I've written what follows. This experience is not meant to be hoarded—it's meant to be spread around.

I'll be offering you sixteen suggestions for keeping a journal. They have come from my own experiences and from what others have shared with me. These ideas are only a start—there's ever so much more you can do as you expand upon this practice. In the meantime, use these suggestions for whatever they're worth to you. If a particular idea doesn't feel right, don't do it. The key is simply to keep obstacles to a minimum so your writing will flow out of you as naturally as possible.

May that be your experience—may your writing flow. And may it be a gentle influence for helping your life flow too.

Jim Miller

How do I know what I think
until I see what I say?

E. M. FORSTER

Writing teaches us our mysteries.

MARIE DE L'INCARNATION

The journal is not essentially a confession,
a story about oneself. It is a memorial.
What does the writer have to remember?
Oneself, who one is when one is not writing,
when one is living one's daily life,
when one is alive and real,
and not dying and without truth.

MAURICE BLANCHOT

1

Know that a journal is not a diary.

A diary is a day-to-day record of how you spend
your time. It focuses on the outward events of your life—
where you went and when, what you did and with whom,
what you saw and heard and said. While a diary may include your reflections about anything that's happened, that
is not its main purpose.

A journal is different. It focuses on the writer's
interior life—how you feel about something at the moment,
or what you think about some matter that has grabbed your
attention. It may involve your memories about something
that once happened, or your thoughts about what you hope
will happen. A journal is always personal in nature. It's
written for no one but you. It's an expression of who you
have been, who you are, and who you are becoming.

The French writer Anaïs Nin, who kept journals
from the time she was a girl, described her journaling this
way: "I chose the event of the day that I felt most strongly
about, the most vivid one, the warmest one, the nearest
one, the strongest one." When you journal, you don't
attempt to cover every aspect of your life—you cover what
you want to, what you're led to, what means most to you as
you sit down and begin.

Your journal may bear some similarities to a diary.
You may choose to write in it every day. (Then again, you
may not.) You may refer to what's going on with the day at
hand. (Or you may not.) One practice used in diary keeping
I'd encourage is to date every entry you make. Doing so will
locate your reflections in time and help you monitor those
changes that occur with the passage of time. I write the day
of the week, the date, and the hour at the top of each entry.
If I'm away from home, I note where I happen to be.

People start diaries for many different reasons. Per-

I must write it all out, at any cost.
Writing is thinking. It is more than living,
for it is being conscious of living.

ANNE MORROW LINDBERGH

If I don't write to empty my mind,
I go mad.

LORD BYRON

Look, then, into thine heart, and write!

HENRY WADSWORTH LONGFELLOW

haps a crisis is leading you to write about what's happening around you and within you as a way of getting a firmer hold on yourself and on life. You may be drawn to writing about your deepest longings and innermost thoughts as a way of clarifying yourself or freeing yourself. You may like the discipline of writing creatively about whatever attracts you—a marvel of nature you've come upon, a person you just met, a moment of serendipity you've experienced, an unexpected happening you struggle to understand.

You will have your own reasons to begin writing if you're new to this process, or to continue your writing if it's already a part of your life. If you haven't yet discovered this, you will: journaling is very much like taking a journey. You start in one place, you go awhile, and then you end up somewhere else. You can't always predict what will happen along the way—it's an adventure. But whatever happens, you'll be the wiser and the better for writing about it. And if you're fortunate, you'll be the happier for it too.

So do this: keep not so much a diary as a journal. Let it take shape in the way it wants. Let it grow in the way it will. Whatever else you do, make it no one else's but yours. ▨

Get black on white.

GUY DE MAUPASSANT

※

I never travel without my diary.
One should always have something sensational
to read in the train.

OSCAR WILDE

※

What sort of [journal] should I like mine to be?
Something loose knit, and yet not slovenly,
so elastic it will embrace anything,
solemn, slight, or beautiful that comes into my mind.
I should like it to resemble some deep old desk,
or capacious hold-all, in which one flings
a mass of odds and ends
without looking them through.

VIRGINIA WOOLF

2

Select your writing tools with care.

A journal is not a throwaway. You'll probably keep it a long time, perhaps as long as you live. Succeeding generations may read it. You may carry your journal with you to distant places, and you may use it in a variety of settings. Those are reasons enough to purchase a well-made journal, one that will last. Still, there are more reasons to choose a book that's substantial. Your writings are important—they deserve a worthy home. And chances are you'll be spending a number of hours before those open pages. So make this a pleasurable time you can look forward to in as many ways as you can. Make your journal something you'll be proud of and happy with.

A hard cover journal will better withstand wear and tear. It will also be more comfortable to use if you're not at a desk or table. A book which can lie flat when it's opened is easier to write in, wherever it's placed. It shouldn't be too small—5"x 7" is a good minimum size. Bound books which are 7"x 10" and 8½" x 11" are commonly available and large enough to support one's moving hand. Some people prefer loose-leaf binders so they can organize their pages and insert other types of material—envelopes to hold keepsakes, for instance, or oversize pages for drawings or clippings. Other possibilities include spiral bound notebooks, sketch pads, and handmade books.

Some writers like lined pages, while others prefer unlined. You may change your mind as you go. For many years I used only bound notebooks containing 300 ruled pages. Today I select journals with fewer pages so they're lighter, and I now want the paper unlined so I can sketch if I want to.

Your other choices include white or colored pages and paper that is smooth or textured. While they cost more,

13

*I put a piece of paper under my pillow
and when I could not sleep
I wrote in the dark.*

HENRY DAVID THOREAU

*There is no lighter burden,
nor more agreeable,
than a pen.*

PETRARCH

My pen is my harp and my lyre.

JUDAH HA-LEVI

The mouth is wind, the pen is a track.

GERMAN PROVERB

books made with acid-free, 100% rag paper will weather better. Pages aren't as likely to yellow with age, nor will ink be as likely to fade.

Pens come in even more assortments than journals. There are ball points, rollerballs, and felt tips in a host of styles, sizes, and colors. Fountain pens have made a strong comeback in recent years. A writing instrument should feel right in your hand and it should look right to you as it moves across the page. My favorite journaling pen has a very fine point, uses blue ink, and costs 29 cents at the drug store. The $150 rollerball I was once given on a special occasion doesn't quite work for this purpose.

Some people write in different colors, depending upon the topic—blue for their reflections, for example, black for gathered quotations, red for their dreams. My daughter has a small wooden case which contains crayons, colored pencils, and pastels for those times when she feels the urge to draw or when words alone cannot convey what she wants to say.

Nowadays we dare not forget that some journals are not books at all. When my wife developed a life-threatening disease, she decided she wanted to create a record of what she thought and felt as the weeks progressed. So she chose to write on a laptop computer. It's faster than handwriting for her, and the words seem to flow more smoothly. Also, it was convenient to use as she lay in bed. Her journal is now stored on a floppy disc and sometimes it appears on a monitor, while other times she prints it out on paper. She's not alone—it appears more and more people are taking the technological route.

Whatever writing tools you select, make them suit you, your needs, and your purposes. It matters not a whit what others think. This isn't their affair—it's entirely yours. ▧

God has promised forgiveness to your repentance;
but God has not promised tomorrow
to your procrastination.

SAINT AUGUSTINE

I write when I'm inspired,
and I see to it I'm inspired
at nine o'clock every morning.

PETER deVRIES

If a person would allot
half an hour every night for self-conversation,
and recapitulate with oneself whatever one has done,
right or wrong, in the course of the day,
one would be both the better and the wiser for it.

PHILIP STANHOPE, EARL OF CHESTERFIELD

3

Develop your own writing routine.

Once you're ready to begin, two questions surface:
When will you write? And where?

Some people make a habit of journaling at a set
time—early in the morning, for instance, or in the evening
before bed. British writer Virginia Woolf, who kept a journal her entire adult life, chose what she called "the casual
half hours after tea." Anaïs Nin wrote in hers very late at
night. If you know in advance when you're going to write,
your mind prepares for that time, whether you're conscious
of it or not. This set discipline gives a priority to this task—
it's like keeping an appointment with yourself. The schedul-
ing of these protected times may depend upon various
factors, such as when young children take their afternoon
nap or when you can claim a room all to yourself.

Another method is to write when the spirit calls—
when a feeling suddenly overwhelms you, for instance, or
when a thought overtakes you. Still another is to take
advantage of those interludes that come into your days,
both those you expect and those you don't. I've done many
journal entries while biding my time in doctors' offices,
waiting for something to cook in the kitchen, or during a
coffee break at work.

How often will you write? Weekly? Several times a
week? Daily? Even more often? As you keep at it, you'll find
the rhythm that works for you. Know that it's not unusual
for people to go through cycles in their journaling; some
periods they're more involved, other periods less so. Life
crises may also influence the frequency of your writing. You
may turn naturally and often to your journal when you're in
pain or despair. Then again, you may find that such experiences interfere with your writing.

However often you choose to write, make sure you

All clean and comfortable
I sit down to write.

JOHN KEATS

The mind can weave itself warmly
in the cocoon of its own thoughts,
and dwell a hermit anywhere.

JAMES RUSSELL LOWELL

You do not have to leave your room.
Remain sitting at your table and listen.
Do not even listen, simply wait.
Do not even wait, be still and solitary.
The world will freely offer itself to you
to be unmasked, it has no choice,
it will roll in ecstasy at your feet.

FRANZ KAFKA

give yourself permission to spend time in this endeavor. This is not a frivolous activity—it has real significance for your life.

Where will you write? Perhaps you'll want the routine of going to a familiar spot each time. If that's the case, it will help to choose a room or an alcove you like, a place that's comfortable and inviting. Most people prefer a desk or table to write at, yet some are content seated in a chair or on a couch or even upright in bed.

Some journalers like to ready their space. One woman I know lights a candle before beginning. Another burns incense. One man likes to have a single flower in a vase nearby. Others want meaningful pictures before them, or gentle music around them, or a flickering fire not far away. For awhile my writer's nest was a small drafting table in front of a second story window overlooking a woods. These days I often sit at a desk with a photograph of mysterious-looking clouds at eye level. A favorite easy chair in my den has seen me through a good fifteen years of this ritual.

It helps if your writing space meets two requirements: it's private and it's peaceful. This will allow you to quiet yourself and to concentrate on what flows from within. But privacy and peacefulness can be found in many diverse settings. I've journaled in libraries and coffee shops, on park benches and seaside boulders, in hotel lobbies and airline terminals. I've even been known to write with my journal propped up beside me while driving down highways.

Truman Capote liked to write lying down. Ernest Hemingway wrote standing up. American author John Nichols writes while soaking in the bathtub, preferably quite early in the morning. Thomas Wolfe used the top of a refrigerator, Jane Austin retreated to a tiny round table in her parlor, and Jawaharlal Nehru did rather nicely with a prison cell. The moral to these little stories? You can write about anywhere and anytime you put your mind to it. ▨

*As soon as you trust yourself
you will know how to live.*

JOHANN WOLFGANG VON GOETHE

*I used to write more methodically.
But one does not dress for private company
as for a public ball.*

BENJAMIN FRANKLIN

*The best style of writing,
as well as the more forcible,
is the plainest.*

HORACE GREELEY

4

Make it easy to express yourself in writing.

If your journal is going to serve its intended purposes, you must be able to make your entries as easily and naturally as possible. If you cannot write in your own genuine way, and if you cannot reveal your real self in your journal, then you won't be using this opportunity to its full potential. There are several ways you can help that happen.

Guard the privacy of your journal. Write in the front of your book that what's inside is confidential and not to be read without your permission. Depending upon your living arrangements and your relationships with those around you, you may choose to keep your journal out of obvious sight. You may even hide it or lock it away. If others live in your household, explain to them what you're doing as you journal and why you're doing it. Ask them to honor your request not to read what you're writing. If you become aware that someone else is reading your journal, you won't be as free with what you write. You'll censor yourself.

If you want, you can protect your writings to an extent by using coded language that only you understand. Remember also that you're the one to decide what happens to your journal, not just now but in the future. What will become of your writings should you become somehow incapacitated? Upon your death? Do you want your journals destroyed? Passed on to a particular person? Released at some later date? It's up to you to leave clear directions.

A second way of encouraging your natural expression is to write without becoming bogged down with the specific words you use and how you use them. Can you allow yourself to forget about misspellings, grammatical mistakes, and incorrect punctuation? Will you give yourself permission to write in incomplete sentences and abbreviations? Is it okay with you to use unconventional terminol-

*Even people who sleep in the same bed
dream their own dreams.*

CHINESE PROVERB

*I only wish I could write with both hands,
so as not to forget one thing
while I am saying another.*

TERESA OF AVILA

*The greatest thing in the world
is for a person to know how to be
oneself.*

MICHEL DE MONTAIGNE

ogy to communicate what you feel? Is it okay with you to scratch out and write over? What if your handwriting becomes less than neat as you race to capture an idea before it escapes?

If you allow your journal to be a very human document, filled with imperfections and innocent errors along with truth as you know it and wisdom as you find it, then you can concentrate on getting as close as possible to your thinking and feeling. Another flexibility you can give yourself is the freedom not to be logical at all times, the freedom to contradict yourself here and there. When you write with energy and emotion, inconsistencies sometimes appear. So be it.

Another way to facilitate your journaling is to utilize methods that help you get started in your writing. In addition to the preparations already described, you can "prime the pump" in various ways. Some people jot notes between writing times, reminding themselves about what they want to include. Some begin with *flow writing*. When you flow write, you free associate on paper for a specified length of time. For, let's say, six, eight or ten minutes, you write down whatever comes to your mind as quickly as you can, whether it makes sense to you or not. Afterward you can read back over your words and perhaps select a sentence or an idea you want to expand upon. Or you can simply turn to your traditional reflecting, having been loosened and opened by this exercise.

Whatever you do and however you do it, make it easy on yourself, as French writer Guy de Maupassant said, to "get black on white." ▨

Paper is patient.

GERMAN PROVERB

Paper does not blush.

AMERICAN PROVERB

Paper endures anything.

FRENCH PROVERB

5

As much as possible, express whatever is within you.

Your journal is not a place to hold yourself back. It's the place to write whatever you think, to say whatever you feel, and to preserve whatever you want. In short, it's the place for you to be whoever you are.

Your writing may take the form of reflections. You may focus your thoughts on the events of your days, including those little occurrences that might otherwise go unnoticed. You may contemplate your relationships with others, significant experiences in your life, or events in the world at large. You may play with ideas or expand upon theories. When you write in this way, you ponder. You ruminate.

Your journal is also a perfect place to express your feelings about anything and everything. As you go through trying times, you may vent your anxiety or fear or despair. As you experience losses in life, you may verbalize your sadness or aloneness, your anger or helplessness. You can just as easily pour forth your joy, your gratitude, and your sense of peace whenever such emotions arise.

As you journal in this way, you can say what you're not yet ready or able to say to someone else. One of the entries in Anne Frank's now-famous diary, as she and her family huddled in an attic, hoping to avoid being captured by the Nazis, was this: "I soothe my conscience now with the thought that it is better for hard words to be on paper than that Mummy should carry them in her heart."

Sometimes it's impossible to communicate what you have to say to others. Paula D'Arcy filled her journal with letters she wrote to her daughter, Sarah, first when Sarah was not yet born and later after her tiny life was tragically cut short. It helped this mother to express her deep feelings in these letters which could not be read by her daughter,

I think with my right hand.

EDMUND WILSON

I feel, therefore I exist.

THOMAS JEFFERSON

I can shake off everything if I write.
My sorrows disappear, my courage is reborn.

ANNE FRANK

and it helped others too—those writings have become a popular book, *Song for Sarah*, which speaks to many bereaved parents today.

When you discharge emotions that are pent-up inside, you do what's sometimes called "catharsis." The original meaning for that Greek word is "cleansing," and that's exactly what can happen when you release your feelings into your journal—you cleanse yourself of them. Interestingly, recent research at Southern Methodist University and Ohio State University School of Medicine has documented that this cleansing literally happens when people write down their thoughts and feelings about traumatic experiences they've known. Compared to those who haven't journaled, such people show higher immunity to illness, make fewer visits to physicians, and generally demonstrate improved physical and mental health.

Unquestionably, journaling about whatever is deep inside you is good for you. It's usually good for those around you too. ▨

It is a thorny undertaking,
and more so than it seems,
to follow a movement so wandering
as that of our mind.

MICHEL DE MONTAIGNE

I listen to myself,
allow myself to be led,
not by anything on the outside,
but by what wells up from within.

ETTY HILLESUM

It is only when we forget all our learning
that we begin to know.

HENRY DAVID THOREAU

6

Allow your journaling to lead you.

Just because it's your pen, your paper, and your hand that do the writing, don't assume that you're the one who's always in control here. Or that you *should* be.

As you make a regular place in your life for journaling, you'll find there will be some days when you sit down to write not knowing what will land on paper. There will be other times when you open your book quite sure of your topic, and yet no matter how hard you try, the words won't come. It's only when you go in another direction and your writing begins to flow that you realize that day's topic was to be other than you expected. Still other times you'll be writing in a fluid, comfortable manner only to discover after awhile that you've changed topics along the way—it's as if your pen has developed a mind of its own. Another experience occurs when you read back over a series of past entries and you suddenly see in your writing what you didn't recognize at the time, or you make connections you had missed before.

Your journaling process can have a striking wisdom all its own. It may be humbling for you to realize how little you direct this procedure at times. Yet it's liberating to realize that too. You can stand back and watch what's happening before you, amazed at what you're being shown.

How do you allow your journaling to lead you? By following your inner urgings as you write, whether you understand them at the moment or not. By listening to that voice that can speak from deep within you. By sitting in silence at times, or by meditating or praying or engaging in a guided visualization before you begin. You can also use various forms of creative writing described in Chapter 12. Mostly, you can simply understand that your journal is more than a confidant—it is also a teacher and a guide. ▧

What shame forbade me speak,
love bade me write.

OVID

You never find yourself
until you face the truth.

PEARL BAILEY

The trouble with writing a book about yourself
is that you can't fool around.
If you write about someone else,
you can stretch the truth from here to Finland.
If you write about yourself,
the slightest deviation makes you realize instantly
that there may be honor among thieves,
but <u>you</u> are just a dirty liar.

GROUCHO MARX

7

Write honestly.

No one is absolutely honest all the time. We sometimes stretch the truth to make a point. We may withhold
our real opinion to please others or to avoid making waves.
If we're threatened or frightened, we may speak a falsehood.
Of all places in the world to tell the truth, however, a
journal is the one place where honesty is not just the best
policy—it's the only worthwhile alternative.

It may be hard to write what's true. Some feelings are
painful to acknowledge. Some facts are embarrassing or even
humiliating to admit. Many of us would rather ignore or
hide some of what we've done or what's been done to us.
Let's be clear: you do not have to write about all that you
know and feel. You may choose to leave some parts of your
life unwritten, some of your thoughts and feelings unex-
pressed. But journaling has nothing to do with writing what
you know is untrue. Then you're only trying to fool yourself, and that doesn't work and it doesn't help.

It may take time and effort to make your way toward
the truth. You may find that you get closer and closer to it
with each entry you add. You may discover that the truth
becomes clearer as you become more open and revealing.
You'll probably find that you become more accepting of
yourself along the way, and more accepting of others too.

The more you tell the truth, the less energy you'll
need to expend not seeing what you don't want to see—and
it *does* take energy to hide such things from your view. But
when you tell the truth, you'll have more energy to invest in
seeing the world as it really is, and yourself and those
around you for who all of you truly are. As you do that,
you become freer, and more whole, and more real. Can you
think of a more fulfilling way to walk the earth each day? ▨

It is necessary to write,
if the days are not to slip by emptily.
How else, indeed, to clap the net
over the butterfly of the moment?

VICTORIA MARY SACKVILLE-WEST

It requires a very unusual mind
to undertake an analysis of the obvious.

A. A. WHITEHEAD

A fool sees not the same tree
that a wise person sees.

WILLIAM BLAKE

8

Write to explore the moment.

"What do I have to write about?" beginning journalers sometimes ask. One of the more obvious things, and one of the more important, is this: the moment at hand.

It matters little what's happening or not happening in the present instant. It matters not where you are or who you're with or what you're feeling. What matters is simply that you look carefully and thoughtfully at the moment before you and then write whatever comes. You may concentrate on your perception of that moment, or your response to it, or both. As you journal, you may try to freeze that passing instant, or savor it, or understand it. You may attempt to make that moment yours, or to make yourself more a part of that moment. Whatever you do, go beneath the surface. Delve. Explore.

You may write only a few words or sentences, or you may go on for paragraphs and pages. I've written at various lengths about a sunset I've been watching, a feeling of contentment as I've sat in my easy chair, and the shape of a flower I'd never seen before. I've written about my daughter watching a bug crawl up her arm, about what a friend said as his wife lay dying, and about the bath I gave my wife soon after her surgery for cancer. All that's required is that you fix a moment in time with your writing or typing and enter into that experience a little more deeply—and perhaps a *lot* more deeply—for whatever length of time feels right. This often entails using your senses more fully, so that you see and hear, smell and taste and touch as keenly as you're able, so you feel as sensitively as you know how.

The options are endless. You may write about what looks beautiful or seems magnificent. You may describe the poignant, the exciting, the mysterious, the funny, the depressing. However you do it, compress into words what you experience or witness, either as it's happening or shortly after it's

The true heaven is everywhere,
even in that very place
where thou standest and goest.

JACOB BOEHME

The bliss e'en of a moment
still is bliss.

JOANNA BAILLIE

An old French sentence says,
"God works in moments."
We ask for long life, but 'tis deep life,
or grand moments, that signify.
Let the measure of time be spiritual, not mechanical.
Moments of insight, of fine personal relation,
a smile, a glance—
what ample borrowers of eternity they are!

RALPH WALDO EMERSON

happened. If you'd like to see how others have done this, dip into the reflections of people like Anne Morrow Lindbergh, Annie Dillard, and William Blake. Try the poetry of Emily Dickinson or Jelaluddin Rumi. Then immerse yourself in your own experiences and write in your own way, relying upon your own eye and ear and tongue.

When you're in touch with the moment as a journal keeper, you can be introduced to two paradoxes. One is the paradox that as you step back from a lived experience in order to write about it, you become more engaged in it, more attuned to it. As you remove yourself a bit in order to fathom what happened, you become more involved in it. The other paradox occurs as journaling becomes second nature to you. When that happens, there will be times when you realize you don't have to write about a moment in order to really see it or understand it. Simply being a journaler helps you stay alert to the magic that's always around you. Then that alertness is there *before* you write as well as afterward. Then you're not just *aware* of moments, but you're *fully living* them. Then what you write becomes more like a by-product, and the product itself is the way in which you live. 🞛

The past is never dead.
It's not even past.

WILLIAM FAULKNER

The past sharpens perspective,
warns pitfalls, and helps point the way.

DWIGHT D. EISENHOWER

Remember that there's nothing higher, stronger,
more wholesome and more useful in life
than some good memory, especially when it goes back
to the days of your own childhood,
to the days of your life at home.
You are told a lot about your education,
but some beautiful sacred memory,
preserved since childhood,
is perhaps the best education of all.

FYODOR DOSTOEVSKY

9

Write to explore the past.

Our culture has become so future-oriented that we sometimes unthinkingly ignore our past. That can happen with our journaling too—we focus so much on what's happening now and what we want to happen in the future that we don't give the past its due. Yet the past is terribly important. It influences our present experience in more ways than many imagine.

Everyone's life story comes complete with interesting details, unusual incidents, funny episodes, and unexpected outcomes. Such events shape your life, leading you to be one way and not another, giving you certain opportunities while denying you others. When the stories of these events are lined up in a row, they form your larger story. By spending time with that story, you can find themes you might not otherwise notice and you can make connections you might otherwise miss. You can claim those parts of your life that you're proud of, and you can carry them with you. You can do something different with those parts you're *not* so proud of—you can learn from them, and you can find ways to release yourself from their undue control.

You can explore the past in various ways as you journal. You may write about your remembered events as they come to you, interspersing them among the other entries you make. You may search for them in your memory or let them pop up in your off moments. You may elect to place these stories in a separate journal so you can give special attention to this part of your life, or so you can do more with these writings later on—turn them into an autobiography, for instance.

Concentrate on three aspects of the past in your journal: people, places, and events.

Write about the people who have inhabited your

What a strange life mine has been!

MARY SHELLEY

And now in age I bud again,
After so many deaths I live and write.

GEORGE HERBERT

You need only claim the events of your life
to make yourself yours.
When you truly possess all you have been and done,
which may take some time,
you are fierce with reality.

FLORIDA SCOTT-MAXWELL

life—your parents and parental figures, any siblings and friends, relatives both close and distant. Who loved you, accepted you, believed in you? Who helped you, taught you, inspired you? Did anyone hurt you or hinder you? Who were the favorite people in your life? The most important? The most memorable?

Write about the places that have made up your life. What can you recall about the home or homes where you grew up? What was your neighborhood like? Your school? The places you played? The sites you visited? The spots you vacationed?

Write about the events of your life, including the very first experience you can recall. Often there's a reason it's the first. What have you done that's been fun? What absorbed your interest? What made you proud? What frightened you? What was it like when you were ill? When you grieved? When you celebrated?

Write about your life as the years went by: births and deaths, marriages and divorces, hirings and firings, various comings and goings. Write other people's stories too, if you wish—those of parents and grandparents that deserve to be passed on, or those of events that swirled around you, even if you weren't actively involved. Locate old photographs and learn from them—notice people's expressions, postures, and positions. Perhaps you'll want to place some of these keepsakes in your journal and write about them as well.

The more you open yourself to the past, the more the past will open itself to you. It's a rich resource you can put to use in illuminating and satisfying ways. ▨

I dream, therefore I exist.

J. AUGUST STRINDBERG

We are nearer awakening when we dream
than we dream.

FRIEDRICH VON HARDENBERG

We are somewhat more than ourselves in our sleep;
and the slumber of the body
seems to be but the waking of the soul.

THOMAS BROWNE

10

Write to explore your dreams.

If you're going to use your journal to learn more
about yourself, you'll benefit from including your dreams on
these pages. Why? Because your dreams are a form of wisdom that arises from within you. Some deep part of your
self wants to communicate with your more conscious self.
Above all, that deep part wants you to be well, to be whole.
If you're somehow torn or fractured, it wants to help you
heal. If you're in the dark, it wants to shed some light. So it
sends you messages as you sleep, alerting you to issues that
need your attention and to possible solutions that await
your action.

Dreams can be very unusual creatures. While some of
them seem quite ordinary, others will strike you as irrational
and peculiar, if not downright zany. Some dreams can be
embarrassing or frightening. But however they strike you,
dreams can help you see the world more clearly, and that
includes yourself, others around you, and your relationships
with those others. Your dreams can send you clues about
the past, the present, and sometimes even the future.

Most dreams do not have "right" and "wrong" inter-
pretations. What they mean to *you* is most important, no
matter what they mean to anyone else. A good way to
approach your dreams is gently and patiently. Look upon
this activity more as play than work. Try out different
meanings and see what feels right. If nothing quite fits, leave
a dream alone and return to it another time. Read about the
symbolism of dreams if you want, but trust your inner sense
more than anything.

"I don't dream," you may say. Yes, you do. Everyone
does, and several times a night.

"I can't remember my dreams," you may say. Yes,
you can, if you prepare yourself. Before going to sleep, tell

*I hold it is true
that dreams are faithful interpreters of our drives·
but there is an art to sorting
and understanding them.*

MICHEL DE MONTAIGNE

*The future enters into us,
in order to transform itself in us,
long before it happens.*

RAINER MARIA RILKE

*The dream is the small hidden door
in the deepest and most intimate sanctum
of the soul.*

CARL JUNG

yourself you want to recall what you're about to dream. Place writing materials beside your bed so you can jot down as much as you can when you wake up. Make quick notes about each dream's setting, characters, and action. Note any colors, sounds, words, and feelings you recall. Record only parts of a dream if that's all you have. Write all this directly in your journal if you wish, or enter it all later, working from the notes you made. Word your dream in the present tense, as if it's happening as you write. Name your dream if you want, and give it the first title that comes to mind.

Some people create a separate dream journal. If you prefer to keep your various kinds of writing in the same book, mark your dreams so they stand apart. Once they're on paper, journal about your response to your dreams. What feelings do they bring up? What do you think a particular dream is trying to say to you? Go back over your dreams at a later time—whether it's days later or years later—and look at what you've been dreaming with a fresh eye. See if there's any connection between your ongoing journaling about your awake time and your dreaming.

Look upon your dreams as messengers that want to help you. While you may not always like the messages they bring, they're honest, once you understand them. If an important dream leaves you in the dark, consider talking it over with a close friend or another person you trust. Then return to your journal and write some more, based on that interchange.

Trust your dreams, just as you trust your journal. They will not lead you astray. ▨

*How prompt we are to satisfy
the hunger and thirst of our bodies;
how slow to satisfy the hunger and thirst
of our <u>souls</u>!*

HENRY DAVID THOREAU

*It is not the eye that sees the beauty of the heavens,
nor the ear that hears the sweetness of music,
but the soul.*

JEREMY TAYLOR

*I find letters from God dropped in the street,
and every one is signed by God's name,
And I leave them where they are,
for I know that others will punctually come
forever and ever.*

WALT WHITMAN

11

Give pen to your soul.

Whatever first draws you to start a journal, and whatever engages you each time you sit down to write, it's important to keep in mind that you come to this exercise as a complete human being. Even if it's especially your emotions that pour out on paper, you still have more than your emotions to express. If you tend to stick to thoughts as you write, you still bring more than your mind to this task. You're a whole being—body, mind, heart, and soul. You'll miss a lot if you neglect your soul on these pages.

If you're like many, you may find it hard to communicate with others about your spiritual experiences and feelings. Your journal may be the ideal place to broach that subject. Here you can write *from* yourself and *to* yourself in the same movement, and that can be the first step toward communicating *beyond* yourself. You need not use special language here—usually simpler is better.

What do you write about? The sky's the limit, in more ways than one. You may write about your spiritual urges, your sense of calling, your heartfelt longings. Write about your questions as well as your beliefs, your doubts as well as your hopes. Journal about your gratitude, your joy, your awe. If what you have to say is too deep for words, then use words to say at least that. Content yourself with knowing that some experiences are not destined for paper.

Some people compose prayers in their journals. Some write down the prayers or the spiritual ideas of others, and then follow these with their own reflections. Some write their insights and sensations *following* a time of personal prayer. Some write to God, and others look to see if God is somehow writing them.

One man I know wrote out, over the course of several months, all that he believed as specifically as he

Humanity is the spiritual part of creation.

CHINESE PROVERB

*The soul lets no person go without some visitations
and holy-days of a diviner presence.*

RALPH WALDO EMERSON

*We dream of travels throughout the universe:
is not the universe within us?
We do not know the depths of our spirit—
the mysterious path leads within.*

FRIEDRICH VON HARDENBERG

could. He did that to clarify his faith for himself, but also to leave a testimony of his faith for his grown children and growing grandchildren. I've known several people who have penned their spiritual autobiographies in their journals, concentrating on their experiences of the soul and on the unfolding of their religious and spiritual life. In my own case, my journal demonstrates that the faith I held in my 20's looked rather different from my faith as I enter my mid-50's. The way I practice my spirituality has also evolved, both within the covers of my journal and outside those covers.

Ultimately, it all becomes a seamless whole. The secular and the sacred, the ordinary and the holy turn out to be not all that far apart. They flow into one another, and become a part of one another, for they flow out of the same source—a Source that is far beyond. ▨

Make visible what, without you,
might perhaps never have been seen.

ROBERT BRESSON

To create is divine,
to reproduce is human.

MAN RAY

Know that there is often hidden in us
a dormant poet, always young and alive.

ALFRED DE MUSSET

Imagination is the divine body
in every person.

WILLIAM BLAKE

12

Experiment.

You'll develop your own favorite ways of using your journal. After awhile your routine will become second nature. But if your routine becomes too routine, you'll miss the opportunity of knowing where your spontaneity could lead you. Unlike what some children are taught, it's okay and even good to "color outside the lines" in your journal.

If you're like many, you'll fill your journal with prose, and that prose will be divided into complete sentences and regular paragraphs. Why not take a different approach from time to time? Try writing in poetry. Perhaps your poems will rhyme, and perhaps not. Maybe you'll write in *haiku*—the style of Japanese verse in which each poem has exactly three lines of five or seven syllables each.

Journal as if you were writing in shorthand, leaving out all unnecessary words. Write about yourself and never use the word "I." Or write about your life from the third person perspective, referring to "he" or "she" even though it's about you. That simple shift in wording can sometimes help you see what you wouldn't otherwise see.

Build lists. "Things I like." "My all-time favorite books." "The names that would fit me better than the one I've been given." "The twenty most important people in my life, in order." "The ten biggest losses I've ever suffered." You get the idea.

Write letters. Long ones, short ones, angry ones, funny ones, touching ones—it's up to you. Write people you love, people you want to understand, people with whom you have a bone to pick. Write people who have changed your life. Write those who have died but who live on inside you. You can copy and send some of these letters if you want, but most journalers never do. Such letters are sometimes physically impossible to send, and other times it no

Imagination is more important than knowledge.

ALBERT EINSTEIN

Writing,
when properly managed,
is but a different name for conversation.

LAURENCE STERNE

Every child is an artist.
The problem is how to remain an artist
once we grow up.

PABLO PICASSO

longer makes sense to send them after they've been written—all that was needed was to get the words out in the first place.

Write dialogues. Start a conversation on paper with another person and see where it leads, putting down the first thing that comes to your mind for each exchange. Dialogue with your partner about something that's really important to you. Dialogue with a parent or a child, whether you last spoke with them thirty minutes or thirty years ago. Get more inventive—speak with a part of yourself, like your fear, your creativity, or an addiction. Speak with an experience that won't let go of you, or a dream that keeps calling to you. Go back to these dialogues at a later time and listen in. What can you learn?

Write short plays and include yourself in them, or include someone who talks like you and shares your concerns. Make up stories and see how they turn out. Write fables about issues with which you're concerned.

Draw. Draw your feelings. Draw your memories. Draw what life is like for you today. Use as many colors as you wish. Sketch. Doodle. Cartoon. Paint. Make a splash.

Keep souvenirs in your journal as another way of staying in touch with the events of your life. Use tape or glue. Add envelopes to store things in. Preserve ticket stubs, post cards, newspaper clippings, pressed leaves, vacation snapshots, restaurant napkins, torn-from-magazine pictures that make you feel good—anything you want.

Experiment by writing with your non-dominant hand. Experiment with where you write. Experiment with when you write. Experiment with how long you write.

Just experiment. ▨

I leafed a little through my diary this morning.
Thousands of memories flooded back.
What a rich year it has been!

ETTY HILLESUM

Those who cannot remember the past
are condemned to repeat it.

GEORGE SANTAYANA

Just as a mirror may be used to reflect images,
so old events may be used to understand the present.

CHINESE PROVERB

The past is only the present become invisible and mute,
its memoried glances and its murmurs infinitely precious.
We are tomorrow's past.

MARY WEBB

13

Go back through your journal from time to time.

Your journal is a way to release your feelings, to compose your thoughts, and to unleash your creativity. It's also something more—it's a way to leave your tracks. Every time you journal, you create a record of where you've been, what you've done, and how you've lived.

Sometimes, just before or after I've written in my journal, I leaf back through those pages and look up my entries from the same date one and two years before. Once in a while I'll go back five, ten, and twenty years. The differences I see in the nature of my writings and in the shape of my life can be amazing. Sometimes I'm reminded of matters I've long since forgotten. Sometimes it's hard to believe I wrote what I did, and other times I realize certain essentials have not changed at all.

When you keep a journal regularly, your journal keeps your life. It files away your concerns and your hopes, your sadnesses and your joys through the years. It shows you—in black and white, or in whatever colors you've chosen—how you've changed and the ways you've grown. As you look back, you can say to yourself about various events in your life, "*I really experienced that!*" or "*I survived that!*" or "*I overcame those obstacles!*". You may be surprised with how much you knew even before you knew you knew.

A well-kept journal gives you something with which to work. You can look for the messages that lie waiting for you, both among the words you've written and between those words too. You can search for the meaning in what has happened and what is continuing to happen. You can gather the lessons. You can make informed decisions.

The longer you journal, the more uses you can find for your journal. There are many more uses than you probably first imagined. ▨

The one who gives me small gifts
would have me live.

GEORGE HERBERT

Blessed is the one who gets the gift,
not the one for whom it is meant.

PETRONIUS

The only things we ever keep
Are what we give away.

LOUIS GINSBERG

14

Ask yourself, "Do I want to share any of these words?"

This must be clear at the outset: you have no obligation to share what you write in your journal with any other person, either now or in the future. Your responsibility is only to yourself. As we've already noted, if you begin to write for others, your journal will change character. You'll start to withhold parts of yourself, whether you're aware of it or not.

However, once you've written only and entirely for yourself, might there ever be a time when you would want to share some of these words with another person? Only you can decide if that feels right for you. You won't have to think about it much—you'll know.

I can imagine how a person might choose to read a piece of their writing aloud to another as a way of communicating as clearly and honestly as possible about something that has deep meaning or real importance. I can imagine how a particularly vivid passage might be copied in a card or letter to another, or in a longer writing one might do for oneself or for others, even many others.

When my daughter turned 20, I created a journal for her as a gift. I went back through my journals and photocopied selected passages in which I wrote about her as she grew up and about my life with her through the years. Included were incidental moments, humorous anecdotes, and personal reflections she had never known. Dated and placed in order in a handsomely-bound book, these short compositions formed another part of her story that she has come to treasure.

Will you share in your own way? It's up to you. Whatever you decide is right. ▧

Against the disease of writing
one must take special precautions,
since it is a dangerous and contagious disease.

PETER ABELARD

It is better to be able
neither to read nor write
than to be able to do
nothing else.

WILLIAM HAZLITT

How can you sit down to write
until you have stood up to live?

HENRY DAVID THOREAU

15

Don't let your writing get in the way of your living.

The 19th century French author Honore de Balzac once wrote, "I am a galley slave to pen and ink." As a journaler, don't let that happen to you. Don't be so caught up with your writing, and with your need to spend long hours in writing, that your journal becomes a replacement for truly living. If your journaling gets in the way of your relationships with others, then it's not working as it ought. If you become more interested in getting down on paper what happens to you than in really investing yourself in those happenings, you'll be neglecting your birthright to really participate in all that life holds for you.

In addition to all that's been named about what journaling can offer you, it can offer you this: a respite—the chance to step back from life, and to give yourself a break from the demands and responsibilities that bear down upon you, if only for a few minutes. You can carve out an oasis of calm or of hope, a safe place where feelings are allowed, or whatever kind of refuge you need. But the purpose of your journal is not to help you retreat from life permanently. It's to help you return to life more refreshed, more centered, perhaps more energized and more at ease.

At its best your journal will lead you, not *away* from life, but deeper *into* life. Not more removed from those you love, but more in touch with them. Not more distanced from yourself, but more in tune with who you're being called to be. ▨

*Every person must go to the mill
with their own sack.*

ENGLISH PROVERB

*Go to your bosom, knock there,
and ask what your heart doth know.*

WILLIAM SHAKESPEARE

*It always comes back to the same necessity:
go deep enough and there is a bedrock of truth,
however hard.*

MAY SARTON

*It is a delicious thing to write,
whether well or badly.*

GUSTAVE FLAUBERT

16

Whatever else you do, make this experience entirely and uniquely your own.

In his book *A Lesson in Dying*, Ernest Gaines tells the story of an unschooled African American man named Jefferson who's been unjustly accused of killing a shop owner in a small southern town in the 1940's. During the trial his own lawyer describes Jefferson's life as "no better than that of a hog." Convicted by an all-white jury, he is sentenced to death. Jefferson's closest relative, his god-mother, realizing nothing can be done to reverse the sentence, harbors a driving desire that Jefferson go to his death walking fully upright as a man, and not as if he were no better than an animal. The town's new college-educated teacher, Grant, is reluctantly pressed into service to help.

Most of the book revolves around how these two men, so different in so many ways, slowly develop a relationship and how Jefferson changes as his day of execution approaches. Along the way, Grant gives Jefferson a blank journal in which he can write his thoughts during his final weeks. That journal is presented in its entirety near the end of the book. With his limited education, Jefferson writes with no understanding of capitalization or punctuation. His vocabulary is extremely limited. He spells only phonetically. Despite all this, his journal is the most eloquent part of the entire book.

Jefferson is real as he writes. He's honest. And he's obviously growing in his awareness of who he is as a human being. He stands tall in the reader's eyes—and in his own—as his journal comes to an end. Grant, the school teacher, stands just as tall when the journal is passed on to him as one of Jefferson's last acts.

Jefferson's writing serves as a reminder to anyone who starts on this journey called journaling.

A person who writes well
writes not as others write,
but as that person alone writes.

MONTESQUIEU

The one who knows others is wise.
The one who knows oneself is enlightened.

LAO-TZU

It is by teaching that we teach ourselves,
by relating that we observe,
by affirming that we examine,
by showing that we look,
by writing that we think,
by pumping that we draw water into the well.

HENRI-FREDERIC AMIEL

Whoever you are, you will benefit from writing about your thoughts, feelings, remembrances, and hopes.

Wherever you have gone and whatever you have experienced in life, you have a story that is worth being told.

Whatever your level of intelligence and whatever the extent of your education, you have the ability to communicate what you know to be true.

Whichever words you use and however you spell and punctuate them, if they're *yours*, that's all that's needed.

However creative you feel, you're creative enough, and however artistic you are, that's exactly the right amount for whatever is yours to pass on.

However your words sound when you read them aloud to yourself, if they're honest and they sound like you, there's nothing more to ask.

However your thoughts flow onto the page, if they flow from you, then you've done as much as any journaler has *ever* done, whoever they are, whoever they have been.

So journal, and be yourself as you journal. Write in your own words, with your own voice, and your own understanding. Write as only you know how. Your life will be the richer for it, and the fuller, and the freer. Just as you will be. ▨

Risk! Risk everything!
Care no more for the opinions
of others, for those voices.
Do the hardest thing on earth for you.
Act for yourself.
Face the truth.

KATHERINE MANSFIELD

Thus it is that I have now undertaken,
in my eighty-third year,
to tell my personal myth.
I can only make direct statements,
only 'tell stories.'
Whether or not the stories are 'true'
is not the problem.
The only question is whether what I tell
is <u>my</u> fable, <u>my</u> truth.

CARL JUNG